I0159631

ACKNOWLEDGEMENTS

This book is dedicated to those who are the survivors of those who closed the door on life by choice, whether knowingly or unknowingly due to its perceived unbearable pain. The full title of this book is
Usher in the Sun, Poetry after Suicide, Written through Distorted Lenses, Chasing after Understanding, Climbing the Ladder Back to Hope.

Above all, I acknowledge and give thanks to the Creator Himself through whom all things are possible, especially His gift of guiding someone to a place of humbled peace with something such as life altering as this.

Dear Readers,

I also want to acknowledge that the majority of these poems were written in 2007 and shortly thereafter. That is when my own journey as a survivor of someone very close who committed suicide began,
and, though I feel light years removed from those initial days of that unnamable internal chaos, I am a traveler still and know I always will be.
I hope sharing this internal poetic audit with you
will somehow be meaningful to you.
Writing it has been meaningful indeed
to me.

Thank you for reading my books.
You are who make it all worth the effort. I love you!

USHER IN THE SUN

Peggy Eldridge-Love

Poetry after Suicide

Written through Distorted Lenses

Chasing after Understanding

Climbing the Ladder Back

to Hope

Heal The River

I am busy with alive,
inhale, ingest.
exhale, excrete,
and for what?
For not,
or for what.
I am busy with tick,
tock, wind,
buzz, alarm,
and just why?
Time saved,
or time lost.
Suppose I don't.
Then what?

2007

The Stretch
(written 5/9/07)

I understand - now – so
I unclench.
We no longer head in
that direction
though I do not yet know
another.
Senseless to resist - still – so
I unfurl
from my fetal curve
 to stretch.
Trust? So I say. Truth?
So I hope.
You did not ask
this time.
I am reminded to be still.
To wait.
Now.

You've Got Mail

We send words at light speed thought to imprint
truth, sprinkle care, exchange the inner scrapings
from the linings of our hearts by way of @,
only @ lacks those five senses that
bond us in reality.

You-at-you.com is not you. That @
cannot eyeball and search the soul
that maybe needs your touch, yearns
for your smell, desperately needs the taste of
your mother, sister, brother, friend or lover's
kiss on their forehead or their lips.

We pick tones to designate, to assign
name, rank, or importance to the call made
or received as though they were faces
we can read like a map that leads
to the source being at the other end.

Though It may flip, snap, sing -- it is not you.
It may not signal a flickering light in a
broken spirit, quicken a sixth sense
of a waning desire to win, or smell
when a demon of hopelessness is
in residence and possesses the keys.

We are not electronic souls that can
be tended, fed, nourished by way of
light waves sent with good intentions.
Go, touch, feel, taste and smell...
See ...
Today.

2007

EavesDropping

i hear them in the distance screaming obscenities
at a loss for better words to say the same thing:
i love you
you've hurt me
make it better.

i see them in their grotesque dance of duck and
dodge,
the only way to find themselves in each other's arms.

i despise them for their weak sick determination
to try to keep the music going with distorted lyrics:
i used to
think so but
not anymore.

i shut them out with the close of my ears, window
slammed down hard against their brokenness.

i hurt for them as they waste life and spill time
across invisible borders that warn:
love bends
love gives
or love breaks.

2007

Fault Line

He fled when I needed him most,
ran from my brokenness, hid
from my pain.
I needed tender.
He gave disdain.
I needed tolerance.
He gave harsh reprimands
when small things
I once dealt like a winning hand
slipped through the cracks
split by the fault that opened
in my head.
I won't always be needy.
He won't always be loved.

2007

Birds and Bees

First a nibble, then a gnaw,
aggression builds,
demands rise,
survival must be
satisfied
by the return of
lust for --
passion in--
the copulation
required to sustain
the living.

2007

A Scribe's Prayer

Enlarge our tents Lord,
stretch the reach of our ropes
so that we might usher in
those seeking the shelter
of Your perfect peace.

Order our steps, embolden
our voices so they may resonate
above the din of dissolution
and broadcast the sameness
of Your never-ending love.

Give us wisdom Lord
to know Your blessings, Your gifts
are poured out on us because
You know we will use them
to further Your Kingdom on earth.

Give us today the bread
of Your purpose for our lives.

Next Window

They tore down the old Watkins Drug
where mother would stop on a
Saturday afternoon to buy us tonics
with names like Beef, Iron and Wine.

There is a hole in the ground where
Watkins used to be and though
there is a fence around it I wanted
to jump into that hole and scream.

I was sick for a week when they tore
down the Dairy Queen a block up the
street from Watkins where we'd
pull in when we left and giggle

when Daddy would peer over the
backseat and take our orders
then smile and wave at everyone
as he took those long, strong strides

on his way to the window with
one of us tagging along, one of
us changing our mind about
the chocolate topping, now wanting

it to be butterscotch, and the

other just happy with whatever
she would get as long as
we were all together on Saturday.

I don't live anywhere near the old Watkins
nor the old Dairy Queen part of town
anymore, but they were my landmarks
of wholeness, proof it once existed

even though it is gone now just like time
has gone and left me lonely for the agape
that grew me on those humble streets
now being prepped for million dollar lofts.

Perfection

I thought looking down I might find
what I'd lost buried in the tall
green grass of that famous summer
when a perfect sun allowed
a perfect wind to send
a perfect breeze that
blew you into my heart.
But it was only when I started
to look up - again - did I
once more comprehend that
there is but one
perfection.

2007

Move Your Toes

Forgive me, but my
discerning spirit quakes
when you keep thrusting
that plate forth between
each self-serving word
you have so cleverly
curved to buzz and deceive
those who so desire
to believe in
your unholy scheme.

Some would call it
greed that is at the
root of those deceived,
but some just are
in need of hope having
worshiped dope before
getting hooked on
you with your crafty
lies that you
synthesize to rhyme.

Woe be unto you,
cause to tell the truth
being in your shoes
comes with weighty
dues that will
make you rue the
day you thrust that plate
in the way of His

hungry, broken, searching
few confused by you.

2007

A Tree Stump

A tree stump marks Uncle's grave.

Tales of his refusal
to be held hostage
by his tinted skin
echo still across the delta,

fables told over campfires that hiss
with marshmallow drippings
extended on oak switches,
held by stubby brown fingers that

belong to wise
tiny black eyes that
wisdom somehow
kissed from the cradle.

They know why a
tree stump
marks
Uncle's grave

and why he swung high
upon that summer breeze
an ornament dripping his own

release before locals who

would never again sleep,
at least not in peace
without wind howling
through broken rest

whispering "I am here
to attest
never again.
No, never again."

A tree stump marks
Uncle's grave.

Fall

Butterflies collide with leaves browned
by full circle, anxious to exit,
to begin to fertilize newness below
the buzz of gravity.

Eyes consume transitions without
connection to the hollow
turn that pushes picture through
the filtered memory.

One dance turned upside
counter clockwise for a better
view of the underside of
updrafts in motion.

November 2007

I can sleep now,
eyes closed against the torment
that once held me,
once drove me with such
agony I grew numb
in order to grow cold
enough to withdraw
from the raw truth.

I can rest now,
secure in having done all
that once I promised,
once I vowed
with cross my heart
and hope to die,
but you did instead
leaving me here
raw with truth.

I can smile now,
sometimes when you flutter
across the backdrop
of my memory
laughing, reaching
enjoying life as
I will now, again
knowing I did all

I ever promised

I would.
Rest well, too,
my dearest
until
we meet
again.

2007

_____

Poetry after Suicide

Written through Distorted Lenses

Chasing after Understanding

Climbing the Ladder Back

to Hope

Civil Disobedience

Speaking on the condition of the state of the union
of the state of the people of the state of me
and you
just never was something I thought it
was going to be my responsibility
to do
I thought my call and my mission
and my obligation was steeped in truth
I thought was word worthy and time worthy
to be prosed and plumped, propped up
and spewed.

Wake up! Don't want to but got to cause
full circle spinning like a frenzy makes me
dizzy
Watching them set up, knocked down
seeing children so ripe with rot
they fall
from the tree
and those who aren't see
nooses thrown over limbs
of education as reminders of
things they don't believe
are true.

So, hell, don't want to but got to
pick up this pen and scratch
views
Seen through windows clouded

with cataract covered
eyes
Smelled by noses that have
nearly lost their scent
but
felt by a soul that can
still hear the rhythm of
civil
disobedience
and taste
the bitterness of
history repeating itself
again
and
again
and
again.

2007

Untitled

Drumbeat echoes heartbeat gush
that nearly chokes on
rush of blood pumped with
thunder thrusts through
billions of live cells in
this deep well of rudimentary
memory.
That I knew you never occurred
while at first I searched
yellowed pages, black ship
ledgers, gritted through
my anguish of lack
of the who, the where,
that us.
Spaces in between my pause
I could not place
lifted me momentarily
from misadventure, wrong
turn, bad choice,
to higher heights
unbidden --

so I thought.
You, them, all, gathered
in unity, in prayer,
in ancestral streams
of consciousness
imbedded in the echoes
of drumbeats that

pump heartbeats
that cause
pause

2007
_____

Specter

He bypasses me as though I am not a poet
saturated in Dante journeys
testing latitudes
crawling under boundaries
to make room for
the next word
that has broken water.
His frump, turned up nose uses silence
as his weapon of disdain
to dismiss
by ignorance like
a child pumped
with bully vibrato.
I wanted his notice as sanction of my right
to toss mine with his
and theirs
whose scholarly letters glistened
though unspoken
in a room where eight hundred pound
gorillas could not hide.
I wanted almost to rent my garment
tear my hair
slit my throat
spill my insides
for unrequited desire
until he turns in my direction
and I realize
he is not there at all.

U A N T Cht

Slap it with attitude
nailed on tin
to state your universe
out spins his,
cross-legged redundancy
leaves an itch,
mutilation your butcher's touch
some might say an edge,
but truth be known
you simply hedge
your polar rage
on chalk board
slabs that once
taught you
how to
be you.

Raw Meat

Never know when, just that
raw meat will bleed long after
life has left it.

The Heretic

Thoughtless little upstart,
he snatched a sliver of hope
from a hanging vine
and swung his bony little ass
into the middle of that
hard, cold jungle
and let out a terrified scream.
You heard, having foraged there,
having hacked and hoed,
dug and clawed a path
through enemy territory,
and you came to his rescue.
He was kin, after all,
and you were wiser than most.
Respect lingered there for you
in the midst of that hell
where no black man should
have been able to dwell,
so your word was enough
to buy him a moment
your promise enough
to buy him a tomorrow.
He swung back through
the tangled vines, back
to this world where his
slime oozes through his
heretic pores as he lies,
denies you were there
to pled his passage.

But he has not yet felt
the tightness of the
tangled vine around his
ungrateful throat, nor
the tug of those who
took your word he was
worth your sacrifice.

Through to the Other Side

Seeing through to his hollowness,
I ache. He doesn't want me to,
see him, that is. Others don't.
They want him to be who he dreams
of being, but isn't.

I taste the fears that startle
him awake when truth
slips between the artificial
layers even he
has grown to believe.

Why should I feel such guilt
knowing there is no one to tell,
even if I want to. I don't.
I wish instead to be snagged,
converted by his glow.

I have been wrong I think
somewhere some time, but not
about this. Ever. He doesn't want
me to, see him, that is. And,
perhaps in reality, I don't.

2008

Cave Proverb

The promise of a few moments' sun
was stronger than evolution
than the rudimentary wisdom
that up turned bellies
were bound to become
someone's dinner.

_____

The Equator's Sun

He is a kiss of the equator's sun against a cool
Pacific breeze.
Intended, yet a surprise, come too soon,
but right on time.

Neither knew what drew them,
any more than they knew what
repelled them

only that once
upon a time
love demanded their obedience.

He was the gift left unwrapped when the guest had
gone.
Intended, yet a surprise, come too soon,
and right on time.

He is the kiss of the equator's sun,
the hint of the days
before

and the days to come
in the simplicity
of his understanding

love
demands
our obedience.

He is the sound of a cool
Pacific breeze,
the kiss of the equator's sun,

an intention
come too soon
yet right on time.

2008
_____

"Pink Chanel"

show me how it is done
when what undergirds
buckles, crumbles
betrays as an 8mm rolls,
records the mad
scramble to retrieve
the blasted pieces
of who he used to be.
i do not have white gloves,
a pill box hat, or a
bloodstained pink suit
by Chanel to show
the world my dignity,
but my stone face
does its best to
mimic you.

Weeping Willow

simple sounds startle.
songs sang send
sad scenes skating,
sailing, silhouettes
shouting

anguish against anger
after answering
awful arching agony

written wantonly within
windows wide with woe
while weeping willows weep.

2007

Illegal Immigration

Browned by equatorial sun
to toast the red days in lush green brush,
where rudimentary rhythms aided
strong rough hands
that beat grain into meal into life,

how could they know the
envy that would await them
on the other side of the long
green waters that came to suck them
into barren lands in need of
strong rough hands
that could beat grain into meal into life?

Of a truth, it was their brown
God-etched perfection
that stirred the jealous,
that drove the frenzy,
that beat life out of those
strong rough hands

that longed only for
lush green brush,
beneath a red equatorial sun,
accented by rudimentary rhythms
and the evolution birthed
in pigment kissed by melanin
to absorb nature's
incandescent refractive truth.

2007…when it seemed time stopped

ABOUT THE AUTHOR:

Peggy Eldridge-Love is a Missouri based poet, playwright, screenwriter, and novelist. Her published and produced works as Peggy Eldridge-Love include *The Knoll Frames , You Beckon, Two People, Loving Buddy, Peach Seeds, Holding It Together with Band-Aids and Safety Pins*, and her poetry is included in Poets and Artists, OCHOS, Denver Syntax, Mused, PoetsArtists, and the Mipoesias Chapbook Series. Under the pen name Tess Allen she is the author of Ebooks *His Wife's Diary (Love Bites), The Jewel Thief (Love Bites), The View from Suite 2100, The Trilogy: A Diary, A Thief & A Secret,* and *A Bundle Tied in Red.* Her official website is www.peggyeldridgelove.com. She is also a non-fiction contributor to publishing and writer related zines, newsletters, and journals.

Follow Peggy on Twitter @Plove413

www.ingramcontent.com/pod-product-compliance
Lightning Source LLC
Chambersburg PA
CBHW030311030426
42337CB00012B/666